Author:

Colin Hynson was born in London in 1962. He studied at the Universities of Manchester, Perugia, and London. He writes history and science books for children, and works on television programs for teachers. He lives in Norfolk with his wife Rachel and children Anna and Ben.

Artist:

David Antram was born in Brighton, England, in 1958. He studied at Eastbourne College of Art and then worked in advertising for fifteen years before becoming a full-time artist. He has illustrated many children's nonfiction books.

Series Creator:

David Salariya was born in Dundee, Scotland. He has illustrated a wide range of books and has created and designed many new series for publishers both in the UK and overseas. In 1989, he established The Salariya Book Company. He lives in Brighton with his wife, illustrator Shirley Willis, and their son Jonathan.

Editor:
Stephen Haynes

Editorial Assistant:
Mark Williams

Published in Great Britain in 2007 by
The Salariya Book Company Ltd
25 Marlborough Place, Brighton BN1 1UB

ISBN-13: 978-0-531-18744-9 (lib. bdg.)   978-0-531-13926-4 (pbk.)
ISBN-10: 0-531-18744-6 (lib. bdg.)   0-531-13926-3 (pbk.)

All rights reserved.
Published in 2008 in the United States by Franklin Watts
An imprint of Scholastic Inc.
Published simultaneously in Canada.

A CIP catalog record for this book is available
from the Library of Congress.

Printed and bound in Shanghai, China.
Printed on paper from sustainable forests.
Reprinted in MMXVIII.
12 13 14 15 R 20 19 18

SCHOLASTIC, FRANKLIN WATTS, and associated logos are trademarks and/or registered trademarks of Scholastic Inc., 557 Broadway, New York, NY 10012.

You Wouldn't Want to Be an Inca Mummy!

Written by
Colin Hynson

Illustrated by
David Antram

Created and designed by
David Salariya

A One-Way Journey You'd Rather Not Make

Franklin Watts®
An Imprint of Scholastic Inc.
NEW YORK • TORONTO • LONDON • AUCKLAND • SYDNEY
MEXICO CITY • NEW DELHI • HONG KONG
DANBURY, CONNECTICUT

Contents

Introduction

Y ou are the Sapa Inca (which means "the only emperor") —ruler, by the end of the 15th century, of one of the biggest empires ever known. From your capital city of Cuzco, in what will later be called Peru, you rule over 12 million subjects, and every single one of them is expected to obey your every command—immediately and without question. Your empire has no iron, but it does have plenty of other metals—especially gold.

As well as being emperor, you are also the son of the Sun God, the most powerful god worshipped by the Incas. This means that anybody who disobeys you is not just your enemy, but an enemy of the gods. That is why you are merciless, and punishment is swift and deadly. However, you generously reward those who are loyal to you.

Being the son of a god means that you can never, ever die. One day your body will stop moving—you will stop breathing and doing all those other things that living people do—but, according to Inca belief, you will still be alive. You will be mummified, and will continue to play an important part in Inca life.

Map showing the Inca Empire around AD 1525

Know Your Place

Inca Society

In an empire as big as yours, it's essential that everyone knows who they can give orders to, and who they must obey. Otherwise there would be chaos, and the whole empire would start to collapse. Even though you're the son of a god, you can't do everything yourself, and you can't personally give orders to 12 million people. You rely on your brothers, uncles, nephews, and cousins to give you advice and to make sure that your orders are carried out. Many of them are governors in different parts of the empire. You need to know what's happening throughout your vast empire, and the governors act as your eyes and ears.

OFFICIALS. After your relatives comes a group of less important nobles called the *curacas*. They are the officials who make sure that everyone carries out your orders. They do not pay taxes, and their sons are given a good education.

HEADMEN enforce your laws in every village.

ORDINARY PEOPLE. You never have any contact with them. They just work, pay taxes, and fight your wars for you.

Ordinary people

In about 1450 the Sapa Inca Pachacuti simplified the laws of the empire and left it up to the curacas to pass judgment in court.

It wasn't me— honest!

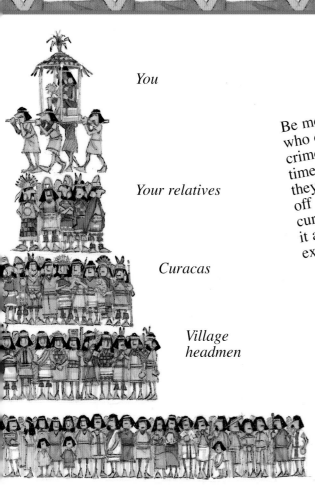

You

Your relatives

Curacas

Village headmen

Be merciful to those who commit minor crimes. The first time they are caught, they can just be told off in public by a curaca. But if they do it again, feel free to execute them.

Handy Hint

I'll work harder next time!

Crime and Punishment

IT'S FINE TO REWARD people for obeying your orders, but you also need people to be afraid of your power. There are no prisons in your empire, but criminals can be executed in several different ways: by being stoned, strangled with a rope, or thrown off a cliff (right).

Your subjects can be executed for murder, breaking into a temple, damaging a bridge—or just being lazy!

Expanding the Empire

You have to make sure that you hold on to your existing empire. You need to keep it stable and put down any rebellions. But you also have a duty to make your empire bigger. Sapa Inca Pachacuti was able to create this vast empire because his enemies could not unite to resist the advance of his army—so he was able to pick them off one by one. Some people accept the Inca as their new rulers without a fight. Those who resist are shown no mercy.

Inca Weapons

Slings

Clubs

Wooden swords —the Inca have no iron, but wood can be deadly if you know how to use it.

The Inca Army

The army that you command is made up of ordinary farmers. Every part of the empire has to send troops to fight for you when you need them. You also have a personal bodyguard of about 10,000 soldiers. You can rely on these soldiers completely. You feel safe when they are around.

Handy Hint

Always give your enemies a chance to surrender before a battle. If they do, reward them. If they don't, you know what to do.

BOOTY captured from defeated villages is carried back to Cuzco (your capital city) by captured slaves.

BE RUTHLESS with defeated armies. Cut their heads off, turn their skulls into drinking goblets and their teeth into necklaces. Some captives are paraded through Cuzco so that you can tread on their necks as a sign of victory.

I'd give my eye teeth for a necklace like that.

Living Like a God

Your clothes are made from the best cloth and wool available. You wear new ones every day, and once you have worn them they are burned. To show your authority you wear a *mascapaicha*—a multicolored braid—around your head. From this hangs a *lautu*, a red fringe with red tassels. Your ears have been stretched with the weight of precious metal jewelry. Nobody is allowed to have bigger ears than you.

Chosen Women

SPECIALLY SELECTED women have been trained from the age of ten. Some become priestesses, some marry noblemen, and the rest become your wives. It is a great honor for their families.

Your personal golden goblet and plate. You drink chichi, *a beer made from maize.*

Anybody coming toward you has to show proper respect. They must lower their heads, go barefoot and carry weights on their backs to make them bow down as they approach.

Any food you leave is burnt as an offering to the gods, just like your clothes.

YOUR CLOTHES are woven specially for you by your Chosen Women.

THE MOST IMPORTANT WOMAN in the empire is your sister, who is also your wife! Your son will become the next Sapa Inca.

Handy Hint

Make sure your Chosen Women know their duties. One of them has to pick up any hairs that fall from your clothes and eat them.

A small token of my esteem, my lord.

Worshipping the Gods

As well as being the son of the Sun God, you are also the chief priest of the whole Inca Empire. You have to lead important religious ceremonies every single day. Constellations, representing animals such as llamas and pumas, have to be worshipped as well. To keep the gods on your side you have to make sacrifices to them. Then, you hope, they will keep your empire safe and prosperous.

Jobs for Priests

SOMETIMES priests use magic and prayer to heal the sick.

SOME PRIESTS are called *orejones*, which means "big ears." Don't worry— they'll never be as big as yours.

PRIESTS ARE ALSO skilled doctors who can make medicines.

Not that well...

Handy Hint

For those who can't afford a llama, sacrificing a guinea pig works just as well.

Every morning a llama is sacrificed to the Sun God. At the beginning of every month, 100 llamas are sacrificed by being thrown into a fire.

Your Own Temple

There are temples all over your empire, but you have one all to yourself. You need a place to worship the gods with only a few trusted people around you. You certainly don't want to mix with ordinary Inca. Never forget that you are the Sapa Inca and the son of a god. Not only do you need your own temple, but it has to be the biggest and the most magnificent in the whole empire.

Gold Everywhere!

YOUR TEMPLE is in Cuzco and it's called Coricancha. It is huge, and the walls are covered in sheets of gold to remind your subjects just how rich and powerful you are. At one end of the courtyard is a huge disc of solid gold representing the sun. On either side of this disc, your mummified Sapa Inca ancestors sit on golden thrones.

Handy Hint

The ears of maize you find in the temple are made of gold and silver and are used in religious ceremonies.

crunch!

Making an offering to the sun disc in your own private temple

The Feast Day of the Sun

The most important day of the whole year is not your birthday, but the Feast Day of the Sun. This always falls on the summer solstice, when the day is longest and the night is shortest. The whole day is spent worshipping the Sun God, Inti. The welfare of both you and your empire depends on Inti coming back every day of the year. It's up to you, as emperor and chief priest, to make sure that this happens.

An Early Start

He'd better not drink all the chichi!

YOU'RE UP BEFORE DAWN to take part in these complicated ceremonies. Priests and nobles from all over the empire have flocked to the city to take part.

HUNDREDS OF LLAMAS are sacrificed to the Sun God. Fortune-tellers examine their hearts to tell you what the next year will hold.

Hmm... could be better...

Handy Hint

Don't get drunk! Make sure that you only take a tiny sip of chichi, or just touch the liquid with your lips.

DURING THE PROCESSION your mummified ancestors are brought out from the temple and carried through the streets so that they can take part in the feast day as well.

How to Die, Inca-Style

How Will It Happen?

As Sapa Inca you live a life of luxury and your every wish is made true by an army of servants and bodyguards. You can also count on the loyalty of your family and the Inca nobility. After all, they are normally one and the same. They depend on you for their wealth and power, so they will do their utmost to keep you safe. Nobody has the chance to assassinate you, and you are likely to live quite a long time. But sooner or later your time will come...

OLD AGE. According to legend, Sapa Pachacuti died peacefully. When he knew he was dying, he divided his jewels and clothes between his sons. They had to look after them as sacred objects. Then he sang a song and died.

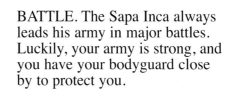

DISEASE. In a city like Cuzco there is always the possibility of plague sweeping through your people. In 1527 the Sapa Inca Huayna died from smallpox, a disease that was brought to the Inca Empire when the Spanish invaders arrived.

BATTLE. The Sapa Inca always leads his army in major battles. Luckily, your army is strong, and you have your bodyguard close by to protect you.

MURDER. The only Sapa Inca who definitely did not die a natural death was Atahualpa. In 1533, after the Spanish had conquered the Inca Empire, Atahualpa was strangled.

When you think your time is near, hand over power to your son in public. Otherwise, there might be a power struggle between your sons by different wives.

Handy Hint

The Empire Misses You

On your death the whole empire goes into mourning. They have lost not just an emperor, but also the link between their lives and the gods that control them. As soon as you are dead, the most important priests and nobles hold a meeting. Their first task is to arrange your funeral. The second is to make sure that your eldest son becomes the next Sapa Inca as quickly and smoothly as possible. If they do not get these two things right, there is a possibility of disorder and even rebellion within the empire.

Your Life Remembered

THE PRIESTS AND NOBLES decide which of your great deeds should be remembered. These will include all of your glorious conquests and triumphs. Nobody mentions your bad points.

Your body is paraded on a litter through the streets of Cuzco. Your loyal bodyguard marches alongside. Your eldest son, who is about to become the next Sapa Inca, follows the litter.

Behind him comes your main wife (that's your sister), then all your other wives. They are all weeping, and as a sign of mourning their faces are blackened and their hair cut short.

Make sure your younger sons are given important jobs—otherwise they might start to plot against the new Sapa Inca.

And then...

THE INCA have no writing, so your life is recorded with *quipus*—bundles of cord with knots in them—by the *Quipu Camayoc* (Keeper of the Quipu).

"REMEMBERERS" who have learned all about your life are sent all over the empire to tell people how great you were.

Drying Out

As soon as your funeral procession is finished, preparations are made to mummify you so that you can continue to take part in the life of the Inca Empire. The first thing that needs to be done is to embalm (dry out) your body. This means that all the fluids inside your body have to be removed. This keeps it from rotting, so you can begin the process of becoming a mummy. There are two ways to embalm your body, using salt or dry air. Both processes are likely to take a few months.

Once you're completely dried out, your body is returned to Cuzco for the rest of the mummification process.

DRY AIR. Your body may be taken up into the high Andes mountains. The air there is dry and cold, and will dry you out like laundry on a clothesline.

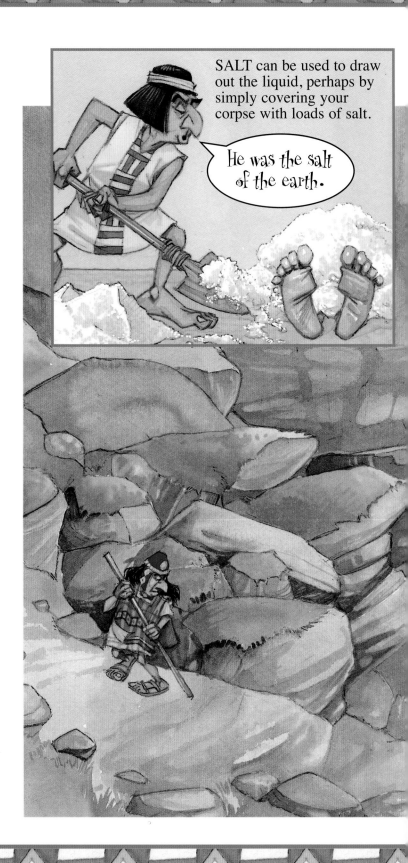

SALT can be used to draw out the liquid, perhaps by simply covering your corpse with loads of salt.

He was the salt of the earth.

The journey through the mountains is long and slow. There are no horses or wheeled vehicles in South America (until the Europeans bring them), so you have to be carried every step of the way.

Crops are planted in steps on the hillside, called "terraces."

Handy Hint

If your body is being dried out in the mountains, make sure there are guards to keep it from being eaten by wild animals.

YOUR DRIED BODY is wrapped in very thick cloth, with your arms across your chest and your knees drawn up. This makes it easier to balance you on your throne. Inside each layer of cloth are offerings to the gods that also provide you with food and clothing. Your royal robes go on top.

23

You Are Not Alone

Like all the Sapa Incas before you, you still have a job to do. The fact that your body is dead doesn't mean that you can stop taking part in the running of the Inca Empire. Of course, you are going to need some help to carry on with your work. You will need some servants. They might not be dead at the moment, but they soon will be. Your priests ceremonially strangle your most important servants so that they can continue to serve you even in death.

Willing... and Not so Willing

Handy Hint

If you want people to celebrate your life, make sure there's plenty of chichi (maize beer) to drink.

SOME PEOPLE ACTUALLY VOLUNTEER to die so they can carry on serving you. Priests, nobles, and members of your family all want to follow you in death. After all, it's a great honor for them and for their relatives.

ALL YOUR SONS (except your eldest, the new Sapa Inca) become your courtiers, carrying your body from place to place. For a whole year they parade your mummified body through the streets of Cuzco. A long line of mourners follows behind, and rememberers sing out your great accomplishments.

No Rest for You!

You're dead, you've been mummified, and you've been paraded through the streets of Cuzco. You are now returned to your palace along with the bodies of those who died with you. Because your palace is yours forever, each new Sapa Inca has to build a new one. That's why there are so many palaces in Cuzco. You are served food, washed regularly, and your clothes are changed. Of course, you won't actually eat the food, but it is still served anyway, and then taken away and burned as an offering to the gods.

YOU DON'T STAY in your palace all the time. On festivals and state occasions you are placed on a golden throne in the temple of Coricancha. You also "visit" other mummified Sapa Inca.

It's up to you, son.

YOU GET TO KEEP all your property, including the parts of the empire that you conquered when you were alive. This means that your son has no empire of his own. This is why the Inca Empire has to keep on growing—each new ruler needs to conquer land for himself.

Handy Hint

Make sure you amass plenty of land and property while you're alive —otherwise you'll have nothing when you're dead.

27

Where Do You Go?

CHILDREN WHO ARE SACRIFICED in the mountains to please the gods are guaranteed a place in the "Higher World."

When you were alive you never believed that you would die and go to another place. As the son of a god, you naturally expected to carry on living forever. But not everyone in your empire is as lucky as you. If they all kept on living, the empire would become a very crowded place. So what happens to ordinary people?

The Inca believe in a place called Henan Pacha. This is a kind of heaven where good Inca people go after they die. Although its name means "Higher World," it is actually deep underground.

THEY ARE CHOSEN for sacrifice when they are about 12 years old. It is a great honor for the family.

A PRIEST takes the child to the top of a sacred mountain. At the top the child is placed in a hole in the ground and given a straw mat to lie on.

A DRUG makes them drowsy and they fall asleep. The extreme cold means that they will not wake up again, so the hole becomes a grave and a shrine.

PEOPLE COME TO PRAY and leave offerings of gold, silver, and carved shells. Sometimes the mountain air mummifies the bodies, though they are not mummified on purpose.

Huh—stones again!

CRIMINALS and anyone who has disobeyed you go to Uku Pacha (the "Lower World"). This is also underground. It is a dark and empty place where the dead have nothing to eat but stones.

Handy Hint

Remember that child sacrifice is a great privilege. Only the children of Inca nobles are worthy of it.

Part of the journey to Henan Pacha involves crossing a bridge made of human hair.

Glossary

Chichi Inca beer, made from maize.

Chosen Women Women trained from childhood to be priestesses, or wives to the emperor or noblemen.

Coricancha The Sapa Inca's private temple in Cuzco.

Curaca An official who sees that the emperor's orders are carried out, and is also a judge.

Cuzco The capital city of the Inca empire, in present-day Peru.

Embalm To preserve a dead body by drying it out.

Headman The leader of a village.

Henan Pacha The "Higher World" where the Incas believed good people would go after death.

Inca A civilization that flourished in South America, in what is now Ecuador, Peru, Bolivia, Chile, and Argentina, from about 1100 until it was conquered by the Spanish in the 1530s.

Inti The Inca Sun God.

Lautu The tasseled fringe that hangs from the Sapa Inca's headband.

Litter A bed or seat carried on poles.

Mascapaicha The braided headband worn by the Sapa Inca.

Mummified Made into a mummy.

Mummy A dead body that has been preserved by drying.

Orejón (plural **orejones**) A type of Inca priest, whose ears are stretched by metal weights.

Plague A highly contagious disease that can kill large numbers of people.

Quipu A system of knots tied in strings, used by the Inca to help them remember important events. Nobody today knows how to read them, but it is likely that the size, color, and position of the knots all had special meanings.

Quipu Camayoc The Keeper of the Quipu: the person who knows how to make and interpret them.

Rememberer A person whose job is to memorize the Sapa Inca's great deeds and tell others about them.

Sacrifice To kill a person or animal because you believe this will please the gods.

Sapa Inca "The only emperor"—the title of the ruler of the Inca Empire.

Tax A payment which people must make to their ruler or government.

Terrace A long step or shelf cut into a hillside, on which crops are grown. Terraces are used when the ground is too steep to make ordinary fields.

Uku Pacha The "Lower World" where the Incas believed bad people would go after death.

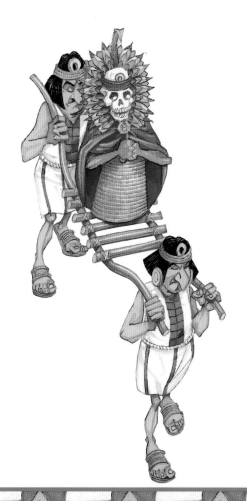

Index